WORLD SERIES
ALL-TIME GREATS

BY ANTHONY STREETER

Book design by Jake Slavik
Cover design by Jake Slavik

Photographs ©: David J. Phillip/AP Images, cover (top), 1 (top); Tony Tomsic/AP Images, cover (bottom), 1 (bottom); FPG/Archive Photos/Getty Images, 4; Bettmann/Getty Images, 6, 10; Archive Photos/Getty Images, 8; Jerry Wachter/Sports Imagery/Getty Images Sport/Getty Images, 13; Rick Stewart/Getty Images Sport/Getty Images, 15; Mark Cunningham/MLB Photos/Getty Images Sport/Getty Images, 16; Adam Glanzman/Getty Images Sport/Getty Images, 19; Bailey Orr/Texas Rangers/Getty Images Sport/Getty Images, 20

Press Box Books, an imprint of Press Room Editions.

ISBN
978-1-63494-868-5 (library bound)
978-1-63494-886-9 (paperback)
978-1-63494-921-7 (epub)
978-1-63494-904-0 (hosted ebook)

Library of Congress Control Number: 2023923231

Distributed by North Star Editions, Inc.
2297 Waters Drive
Mendota Heights, MN 55120
www.northstareditions.com

Printed in the United States of America
082024

ABOUT THE AUTHOR

Anthony Streeter is a former sportswriter who has written for various newspapers. He lives in Columbia, Missouri, with his wife and three kids.

TABLE OF CONTENTS

MATHEWSON

CHAPTER 1
EARLY CHAMPIONS

The National League (NL) formed in 1876. The American League (AL) began play in 1901. Two years later, the winner of each league met in the first World Series. The new championship series quickly became an American tradition. Today, it's also known as the Fall Classic.

Christy Mathewson delivered one of the first iconic performances in World Series history. In 1905, the New York Giants pitcher threw three complete-game shutouts. Mathewson's amazing play helped the Giants beat the Philadelphia Athletics.

Before long, the Athletics were back. They won three World Series titles from 1910 to 1913. **Eddie Collins** was a big reason why. The quick second baseman could do it all. He went on to win one more World Series with the Chicago White Sox. In 34 World Series games, Collins batted .328 while driving in 11 runs.

In 1918, the Boston Red Sox won their fifth World Series. At the time, no team had won more. A young pitcher named **Babe Ruth** helped

Boston win three of those titles. However, the Red Sox sold Ruth to the New York Yankees in 1920. On his new team, Ruth became a home run-slugging outfielder. He also helped turn the Yankees into a dynasty. The team broke through for its first championship in 1923. Then first baseman **Lou Gehrig** joined Ruth. New York's lineup was so feared that it became known as "Murderers' Row." By the time Gehrig retired in 1939, the Yankees had won seven championships.

New York's winning ways didn't stop. By 1962, the Yankees had won 12 more titles.

BOBBY RICHARDSON

The Pittsburgh Pirates upset the Yankees in the 1960 World Series. But New York second baseman Bobby Richardson drove in 12 runs. That's the most in a single World Series. Richardson is the only player from a losing team to be named World Series Most Valuable Player (MVP).

Joe DiMaggio was a driving force behind nine of them. In 199 World Series at-bats, the center fielder recorded 30 runs batted in (RBIs) and eight home runs. **Mickey Mantle** eventually replaced DiMaggio in center field.

Mantle reached the World Series 12 times in his 18-year career. The Yankees won seven of them. No player in history has more World Series home runs, RBIs, or runs scored than Mantle.

Others played key roles for the Yankees. **Whitey Ford** pitched for six championship teams. His 10 wins and 94 strikeouts are World Series records. In 1956, **Don Larsen** threw the first perfect game in World Series history. Catcher **Yogi Berra** was behind the plate. That season was one of Berra's 10 World Series championships. No player has won more.

STAT SPOTLIGHT

WORLD SERIES RECORD

CAREER HITS

Yogi Berra: 71

KOUFAX

32

CHAPTER 2
CLASSIC PERFORMANCES

Sandy Koufax threw a blazing fastball. And just when hitters thought they were ready for it, Koufax nailed them with his curveball. His incredible pitching helped the Los Angeles Dodgers win three championships in seven years. Koufax was named World Series MVP in 1963 and 1965. In those two series, he struck out 52 batters in 42 innings. Opponents scored only five runs on him.

Pitchers thrived in the 1960s. **Bob Gibson** dominated three World Series in this era. His St. Louis Cardinals won two of them. In 1964, Gibson threw 10 innings in a Game 5 win. Three days later, he pitched a complete game to help the Cardinals win Game 7. The hard-throwing ace was named World Series MVP in both 1964 and 1967.

In 1968, the Cardinals ran into **Mickey Lolich** and the Detroit Tigers. Lolich tossed complete games in Games 2, 5, and 7. In Game 7, he earned an epic win against Gibson and helped Detroit take home the title.

Balls rarely got past **Brooks Robinson**. The slick-fielding third baseman helped the Baltimore Orioles reach four World Series and win two. In the 1970 series, he hit .429 with two home runs and six RBIs.

STAT SPOTLIGHT

WORLD SERIES RECORD

STRIKEOUTS IN A SERIES

Bob Gibson: 35 (1968)

Rollie Fingers was a dominant closer. His late-inning work helped the Oakland Athletics with three straight titles from 1972 to 1974. **Reggie Jackson** helped, too. "Mr. October" was known for stepping up in the postseason. He went on to win two more titles with the New York Yankees. In 1977, Jackson hit three home runs on three pitches in Game 6. He also earned his second World Series MVP Award that year.

Detroit won the 1984 World Series. Workhorse **Jack Morris** threw a pair of complete-game wins. But his most legendary performance came in Game 7 of the 1991 World Series. Morris was pitching for his hometown Minnesota Twins. The championship was on the line. Morris threw 10 shutout innings. Minnesota beat the Atlanta Braves 1–0. Then, one year later, Morris won a third World Series. This one came with the Toronto Blue Jays.

WALK-OFF WINNERS

A walk-off hit has decided the World Series nine times. Two of them were home runs. Bill Mazeroski did it first. His Game 7 homer in 1960 lifted the Pittsburgh Pirates past the New York Yankees. Joe Carter of the Toronto Blue Jays did it in Game 6 in 1993.

MORRIS
47
Twins
47

JETER
2

CHAPTER 3
SEEING STARS

The New York Yankees returned to the Fall Classic in 1996. The Atlanta Braves won the first two games. Then the Yankees won four in a row to claim the title. Rookie shortstop **Derek Jeter** had five hits in the series.

The Yankees went on to win three straight titles from 1998 to 2000. Then they added another in 2009. **Mariano Rivera** was around for all five. He became the Yankees closer in 1997. Perhaps no one in history did the job better. Rivera set an all-time record with 11 World Series saves. Two of them came in 1999, when he was the series MVP. Jeter won the award the next year. "The Captain" won fans over with his stellar play over the five World Series wins.

David Ortiz joined the Boston Red Sox in 2003. At that point, Boston hadn't won the World Series since 1918. The slugger hit a three-run homer in Game 1 of the 2004 Fall Classic. Ortiz helped the Red Sox win titles in 2004 and 2007. But Ortiz was at his best in 2013. "Big Papi" recorded 11 hits and six RBIs to lift Boston to its third title in 10 years.

Albert Pujols led the St. Louis Cardinals to championships in 2006 and 2011. The first baseman couldn't be stopped in Game 3 of the 2011 World Series. He went 5-for-6 with three homers, four runs, and six RBIs.

The Giants moved from New York to San Francisco in 1958. Fifty years later, they had

yet to win a World Series in their new city. **Madison Bumgarner** helped change that. The Giants won in 2010, 2012, and 2014. Bumgarner saved his best for last. In 2014, he was dominant in his two starts. Then in Game 7, he tossed five scoreless innings in relief.

Bumgarner gave up just one run in 21 innings pitched in the series.

In the 2020 World Series, Los Angeles Dodgers shortstop **Corey Seager** racked

DAVID FREESE

The Cardinals were down to their last out in Game 6 of the 2011 World Series. But David Freese drove in the tying run on a triple. Then in the 11th inning, he hit a walk-off homer. The hometown outfielder had five extra-base hits and seven RBIs in the series. He earned MVP honors as the Cardinals went on to win Game 7.

up eight hits. Three years later, Seager hit three home runs in the World Series for the Texas Rangers. Seager lifted both teams to championships. And he became the fourth player to win multiple World Series MVP Awards.

STAT SPOTLIGHT

WORLD SERIES RECORD

CAREER EARNED RUN AVERAGE (ERA)

Madison Bumgarner: 0.25

TIMELINE

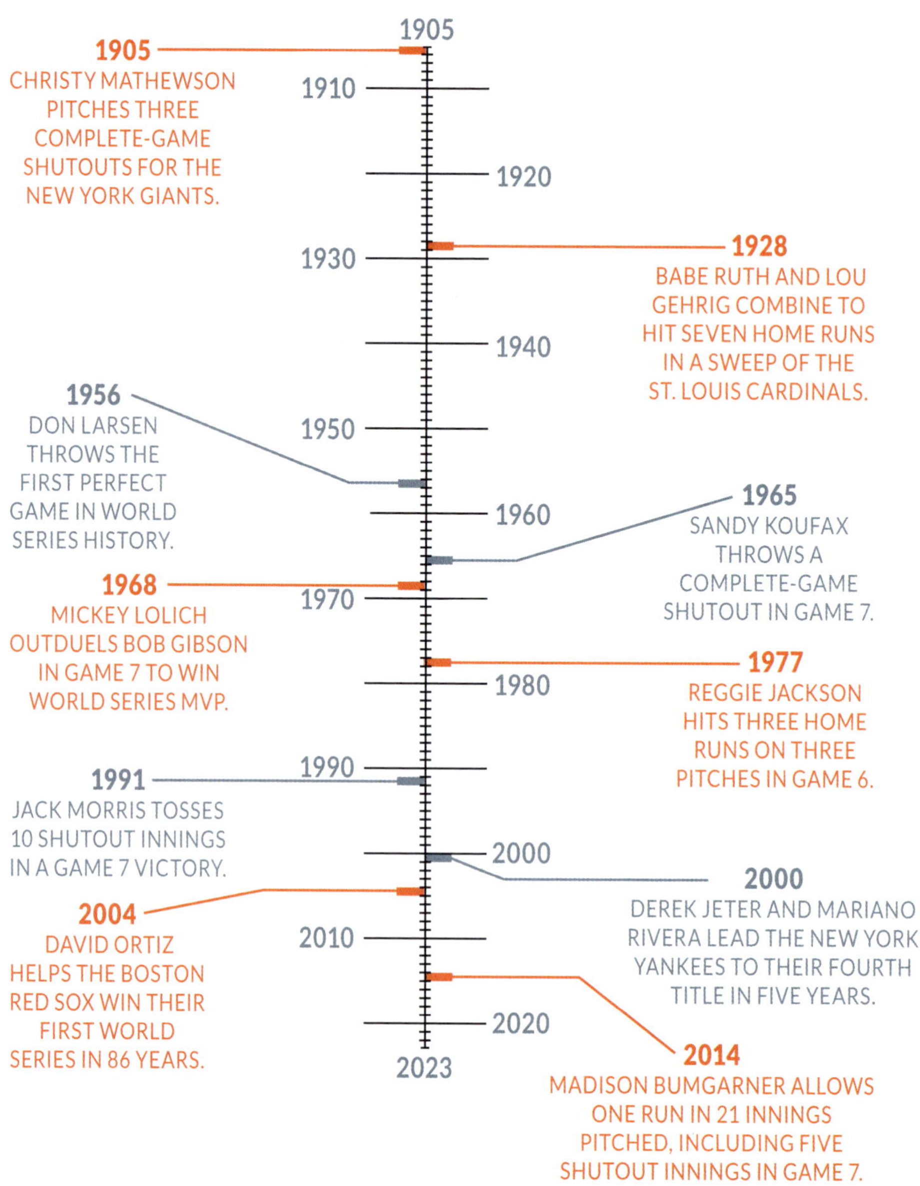
1905
1910
1920
1930
1940
1950
1960
1970
1980
1990
2000
2010
2020
2023
1905
CHRISTY MATHEWSON PITCHES THREE COMPLETE-GAME SHUTOUTS FOR THE NEW YORK GIANTS.
1928
BABE RUTH AND LOU GEHRIG COMBINE TO HIT SEVEN HOME RUNS IN A SWEEP OF THE ST. LOUIS CARDINALS.
1956
DON LARSEN THROWS THE FIRST PERFECT GAME IN WORLD SERIES HISTORY.
1965
SANDY KOUFAX THROWS A COMPLETE-GAME SHUTOUT IN GAME 7.
1968
MICKEY LOLICH OUTDUELS BOB GIBSON IN GAME 7 TO WIN WORLD SERIES MVP.
1977
REGGIE JACKSON HITS THREE HOME RUNS ON THREE PITCHES IN GAME 6.
1991
JACK MORRIS TOSSES 10 SHUTOUT INNINGS IN A GAME 7 VICTORY.
2000
DEREK JETER AND MARIANO RIVERA LEAD THE NEW YORK YANKEES TO THEIR FOURTH TITLE IN FIVE YEARS.
2004
DAVID ORTIZ HELPS THE BOSTON RED SOX WIN THEIR FIRST WORLD SERIES IN 86 YEARS.
2014
MADISON BUMGARNER ALLOWS ONE RUN IN 21 INNINGS PITCHED, INCLUDING FIVE SHUTOUT INNINGS IN GAME 7.

CHAMPIONSHIP FACTS

WORLD SERIES

First played: 1903
Most titles as a player: Yogi Berra, 10
Most titles as a manager: Joe McCarthy and Casey Stengel, 7
Most titles by team: New York Yankees, 27

Stats are accurate through the 2023 season.

MORE INFORMATION

To learn more about the World Series, go to **pressboxbooks.com/AllAccess**.

These links are routinely monitored and updated to provide the most current information available.

GLOSSARY

ace
The best starting pitcher on a team.

closer
A relief pitcher who usually plays in the ninth inning to protect a lead.

complete game
When one pitcher throws every inning in a single game.

dynasty
A team that has an extended period of success, usually winning multiple championships in the process.

extra-base hits
Doubles, triples, and home runs.

perfect game
A game in which a pitcher doesn't allow any batters to reach base.

rookie
A first-year player.

saves
Games that a pitcher finishes when his team is leading by three runs or fewer.

walk-off
A play that ends the game.

workhorse
A pitcher who throws many innings and rarely misses games.

INDEX